Stories to Seniors Sharp

Positive Tales and Trivia to Stay Happy, Improve Memory, Engaged and On Your Toes

Large Text

B N William

Let's be clear—no one's saying you *aren't* sharp. But if your granddaughter handed you this book, she might be trying to tell you something (maybe that you've been a little too grumpy about the weather lately). Don't worry, though. Whether you're feeling sharp as a tack or just want to prove to the family that you've still got it, this book is here to keep you on your toes, with a smile on your face.

Inside, you'll find a collection of positive stories and trivia designed to keep your mind buzzing and your spirits lifted. It's not just about staying sharp—it's about staying happy, engaged, and enjoying a good laugh along the way. Whether you're reminiscing about the good ol' days or learning something new, this book is your trusty companion for keeping those brain cells active and that heart light.

So go ahead, dive into these stories, quiz yourself, and maybe even throw in a witty comeback the next time your granddaughter asks how you're doing. After all, sharp and happy is the best kind of sharp. Let's get started!

Contents

The Drugstore Owner Who Hypnotized His Customers

It's May 1951 in sunny Miami, and life is buzzing with the sounds of swing music, soda fountains, and, of course, the bustling hum of Ralph Pearson's local drugstore. Ralph was no ordinary drugstore owner. Sure, he stocked the usual—aspirin, cough syrup, and cigarettes—but Ralph had a unique "service" that kept the customers coming back, and it wasn't his sale on toothpaste. No, Ralph had a secret talent: he was a hypnotist. And, as it turns out, he wasn't shy about practicing on his customers.

Now, when you think of a drugstore, you probably imagine neatly arranged shelves, friendly chatter, and maybe the smell of soap or fresh coffee. But for Ralph Pearson's customers, visiting his store often meant a trip to another world—literally. Ralph, with his twinkling eyes and soft-spoken charm, had mastered the art of hypnosis and found it to be the perfect way to entertain—and, sometimes, "help"—the people who wandered through his doors.

It all started innocently enough. Ralph had been dabbling in hypnosis as a hobby, mostly for fun. He learned a few tricks here and there, probably starting with the old "stare into my eyes" routine, practicing on friends and family. But as he got better, Ralph realized that his hypnotic powers could work on just about anyone, even his unsuspecting customers. So, naturally, he started offering a little extra "service" along with their prescriptions and soda fountain treats.

Imagine walking into Ralph's drugstore for something simple, like a cold remedy or a pack of gum. Ralph would greet you with a friendly smile, and before you knew it, you'd find yourself sitting in one of those big swivel chairs at the soda counter, listening to his soothing voice. "Just relax," he'd say. "Focus on my voice." Suddenly, you're no longer in a drugstore in Miami — no, you're flying a plane over the Atlantic Ocean, the wind rushing through your hair as you control the aircraft. Or maybe, you're at the same soda fountain, but instead of slurping on a root beer float, you're kissing the person next to you, completely convinced you're in the middle of a romantic moment.

And Ralph? He'd just stand behind the counter, grinning to himself as his customers were transported to wherever his imagination—or theirs—wanted to take them. The whole scene must have been something out of a comedy sketch: one minute you're deciding between gum or mints, the next you're in a hypnotic trance, making airplane noises or puckering up at thin air.

Of course, Ralph didn't stop there. His hypnotic powers weren't just for fun and games. No, Ralph was an entrepreneur at heart, and he saw that his hypnosis could be used for more practical purposes—like curing bad habits. People who wanted to quit smoking started coming to Ralph for his hypnotic touch. He'd put them under, tell them to imagine a life without cigarettes, and when they woke up, many of them had lost their desire to smoke.

Sounds like a win-win, right? Well, not exactly. Ralph soon realized that while his new hypnotic business was helping people, it was also hurting his sales—his *cigarette* sales, to be exact. After all, the more customers he helped kick the habit, the fewer packs of smokes he was selling. "It's cutting into my cigarette sales," he'd complain with a wink, as though curing people's addictions was just a side effect of his main goal—keeping his business thriving.

But Ralph couldn't stop. He had become a local sensation. People flocked to his store not just for medicine or milkshakes but for the chance to be hypnotized by the man with the golden voice. Word spread quickly: if you wanted a break from your daily worries, all you had to do was pop by Ralph's drugstore, and he'd take you on a mental vacation, free of charge (unless, of course, you bought something on your way out).

The best part? No one seemed to mind being hypnotized. In fact, they *loved* it. People would return again and again, asking Ralph to send them off on another adventure or help them break another bad habit. Whether they wanted to fly a plane, kiss an imaginary sweetheart, or simply stop biting their nails, Ralph had them covered.

Of course, not everyone was sold on the idea. Some of Ralph's competitors in the pharmacy world raised an eyebrow (or two). After all, this wasn't exactly normal drugstore behavior. But Ralph didn't care—his hypnotism was harmless, and as long as he had a willing customer, he was happy to help.

Eventually, the novelty wore off, and Ralph's drugstore went back to being, well, a regular drugstore. But for a while, in the spring of 1951, Miami had its own slice of hypnosis heaven, thanks to a man who just couldn't resist taking his customers on a mental joyride.

And really, who could blame him? In a world filled with stress and ailments, Ralph Pearson gave people something much more valuable than a bottle of cough syrup—he gave them a chance to escape, even if just for a few minutes, with the help of a little hypnotic suggestion.

So, the next time you're in a drugstore, and the pharmacist asks if you need anything else, remember: it could always be weirder. You could be sitting there, imagining yourself flying a plane over Miami or kissing the soda jerk. At least your trip to the store won't be quite as... hypnotic.

Miss Sewer Cleaner of 1952: A Crown in the Drain

❧

In October 1951, Gaylia Davis, a 17-year-old aspiring actress from Detroit, made a decision that might raise some eyebrows today—or, more likely, a few chuckles. Gaylia accepted the title of "Miss Sewer Cleaner of 1952," a job title you probably didn't see coming in your morning coffee. But Gaylia? She took it all in stride.

Now, before you wonder why a young woman with Hollywood dreams would dive into such murky territory, there was a catch—one that would've made any starlet perk up. In exchange for her newfound title, Gaylia was promised that her picture would be blown up and featured at sewer conventions across the country. Yes, you heard that right: sewer conventions. She was going to be the glamorous face of... well, plumbing.

But to Gaylia, it wasn't about the muck—it was about the spotlight. With the kind of savvy mindset that only an ambitious teenager could muster, she accepted the title with open arms. "It may be a soggy title," she reflected with a smile, "but if it helps my career, I don't care." And that's the kind of gumption that made Gaylia a legend in her own right. While others were aiming for beauty queen sashes, she was aiming for the stars—even if those stars came with a little bit of sludge.

Gaylia wasn't fazed by the less-than-glamorous nature of her new role. In fact, she saw it as an opportunity, a stepping stone on the way to bigger things. If she had to pose with a plunger and flash her best Hollywood smile next to a manhole, so be it. As far as she was concerned, it was all part of the journey.

And really, who could blame her? In an industry where getting noticed was half the battle, Gaylia was willing to do whatever it took—even if it meant being crowned queen of the sewer. She understood something that many of us learn a little later in life: sometimes you have to go through the muck to get to where you're going. And, if you can do it with a smile, well, that's just the cherry on top—or in this case, the rubber gasket.

Gaylia's story is a reminder that life's titles don't define us—it's what we do with them that counts. So, next time you're faced with an opportunity that seems a little... unconventional, remember Miss Sewer

Cleaner of 1952. She didn't let a soggy title dampen her spirits, and neither should you.

Because if you can wear a crown in the sewer, you can shine just about anywhere.

Wrong Turn into the Coal Mine: A Scenic Detour

In January 1963, a woman driving from Sydney to Melbourne with her two sons found herself on what can only be described as the most unusual scenic route ever. Now, we've all taken a wrong turn here or there, maybe ended up on the wrong highway or found ourselves circling the same roundabout more times than we'd care to admit. But this particular detour? Well, let's just say it had a little more *character* than your average U-turn.

It all started out like any other road trip. The kind where the kids are in the backseat, trying to outdo each other with "Are we there yet?" and "I'm hungry" chants while mom is doing her best to keep calm and navigate the winding roads. Everything was going fine until she took one little wrong turn off the main road. But hey, who among us hasn't made a tiny mistake like that? Of course, when most people make a wrong turn, they end up on a quiet back road or in the parking lot of some diner they weren't planning to visit. But not this mom. Oh no. She ended up on a mountain road that, to her credit, *looked* like it might take her back to the highway. It didn't.

Instead, the road led her straight into what she thought was a tunnel. But here's the thing—it wasn't a tunnel. It was a coal mine. Yes, an actual working coal mine. Not that she noticed right away, of course. After all, tunnels and coal mines can look surprisingly similar when you're trying to keep your kids entertained, avoid potholes, and squint through a pair of sunglasses that might've been stylish but weren't exactly helping with the visibility.

So there she was, driving deeper and deeper into the mine, thinking, "This tunnel sure is long." Her sons, meanwhile, were having the time of their lives. Who needs a theme park when you've got a bumpy, dark, and mysterious "tunnel" to drive through? Half a mile in, they were probably wondering where it was going to spit them out—maybe the other side of the mountain, maybe even a hidden treasure. Spoiler alert: it wasn't a treasure. It was a wooden post.

Smack. That was the end of the road, literally. She ran right into it, and suddenly, the realization hit. This wasn't just any tunnel. This was a coal mine. And as much as she would've liked to throw the car into reverse and back out like nothing happened, there was no getting around that post. Not to mention, reversing half a mile out of a coal mine is no small task.

Fortunately, the coal mine employees were understanding, if not a little surprised to see a family sedan casually parked halfway inside their mine. They gathered around, scratching their heads, probably wondering how on earth a road trip had landed someone in their workplace. But, true to the helpful spirit, they rolled up their sleeves, got out their tow equipment, and hauled her car out of the mine.

And that's how a simple trip from Sydney to Melbourne turned into an unexpected adventure, complete with a few laughs and some really interesting stories to tell at the next family gathering. Because let's be honest, anyone can take a wrong turn into a cul-de-sac, but it takes real talent to accidentally drive into a coal mine.

The best part? She wasn't even phased. Sure, she got a little off track, but in the end, she made it out with a great story, two giggling kids, and maybe a new appreciation for road signs. Sometimes, the best trips aren't about getting to your destination perfectly. They're about the detours, the wrong turns, and the moments you never saw coming. And this was one detour that she—and the coal miners— weren't likely to forget anytime soon.

So, next time you miss a turn, just remember: at least you didn't end up in a coal mine. And even if you did, it's all part of the adventure, right?

Mail-Order Beatlemania: Carol's Postage-Paid Adventure

❧

In June 1966, the world was caught in the throes of Beatlemania, and no one was more swept up in it than 12-year-old Carol Dryden. Like millions of others, Carol dreamed of meeting the Fab Four, but she had something that set her apart—determination and, well, a bit of an unusual plan. You see, while other fans wrote letters or waited outside concert venues, Carol had a much more *creative* idea. She was going to mail herself to the Beatles.

That's right. Carol figured if she couldn't get to London on her own, why not ship herself there? After all, packages arrived safe and sound every day. Why shouldn't she be one of them?

With a plan as bold as it was impractical, Carol enlisted the help of a friend. Together, they found a sturdy box and wrote the address in big, confident letters: "To The Beatles, care of their fan club, London." They didn't waste time on trivial details like logistics—food, water, or, as it turns out, air. Carol was too busy imagining herself bursting out of the box at Beatles HQ, with John, Paul, George, and Ringo staring in awe at her dedication.

So, into the box she went, armed with little more than her sweater and a whole lot of ambition. The plan was simple: her friend would drop the box off at the railway station, and Carol would be on her way to London, where Beatlemania dreams would come true. But, as with most great adventures, things didn't go exactly as planned.

Once inside the box, Carol quickly realized a few things she hadn't accounted for. First, it was hot—*really* hot. Not exactly the kind of cozy she was expecting. Second, she hadn't made any holes in the box. You know, for air. So there she was, in a wobbling box, sweating profusely, and finding herself in a very real battle with her sweater. As anyone who's ever tried to take off a sweater in a confined space knows, it's a struggle. Now, imagine doing that while sealed inside a box, on your way to meet the Beatles, no less.

As the box wobbled back and forth on the platform, drawing more attention than an inconspicuous package should, it didn't take long for a railway clerk to notice. He saw the box shimmying about, like it had decided it was time for a little dance. Curious, he walked over, probably thinking some mischievous prank was at play. What he didn't expect to find was a determined, overheating 12-year-old struggling to peel off a sweater inside.

With the jig quite literally up, Carol was freed from her cardboard fortress. She was red-faced, a little sweaty, and more than a little sheepish. When asked what on earth she was doing, Carol confessed her grand plan: she was mailing herself to the Beatles. She didn't have a Plan B, or even much of a Plan A, really. She admitted that in her excitement to meet her idols, she had completely forgotten to think about minor details like air, water, or how long it might take for her to reach London.

Luckily, Carol's ill-fated journey was cut short before things got too serious, but she did leave behind quite the story. It's not every day someone tries to package themselves to meet a rock band, after all. And while she never did make it to London that way, she became a local legend, the girl who loved the Beatles so much, she tried to mail herself to them.

Looking back, Carol's adventure is a perfect reminder that sometimes our dreams, while ambitious, don't always go as planned. And that's okay. After all, if nothing else, Carol can say she gave it her all—and then some. So next time you're feeling particularly bold, just remember to leave a little room for fresh air in your plan. Or at least avoid wearing a sweater.

The Shortest Boxing Match

It was December 29, 1953, and in Toronto, boxing fans gathered in anticipation for what was supposed to be an exciting match. Among the fighters scheduled for the night was a local boxer named Les Stork. Stork wasn't exactly a household name, but he was ready to give it his all, like any athlete stepping into the ring. Or so everyone thought.

The bell rang, the lights shone down on the ring, and the crowd murmured in excitement as Les Stork made his entrance. But when Stork took one look at his opponent—a man who clearly had a few pounds on him, not to mention a solid reputation—the unexpected happened.

Stork froze, blinked once, and before anyone could even register what was going on, he crumpled to the canvas. Down for the count. Not from a punch, mind you—his opponent hadn't even moved yet. No, Stork had passed out cold just from the sight of the man standing across from him.

The referee, stunned, had no choice but to call the match before it even started. Medical personnel rushed to the ring, and it took a good ten minutes before Stork was revived.

The crowd, at first confused, soon erupted in a mix of laughter and disbelief. What was supposed to be a night of punches and parries had turned into what would go down as one of the shortest—and perhaps strangest— boxing matches in history.

Whether it was nerves, the pressure of the moment, or simply facing an opponent who looked like he'd been carved out of stone, no one knows exactly what caused Stork to faint that night. But his name will forever be linked to a bout where the only knockout punch came from his own imagination.

And just like that, the legend of Les Stork—who saw his opponent and immediately hit the mat—was born.

Bananas Used to Launch a Ship: The Slipperiest Launch in History

It's January 1941, and the world is gripped by World War II, but in Beaumont, Texas, something a little more... fruity is making waves. Amid the shipyards and salty air, shipbuilders are getting ready to launch the largest cargo vessel ever constructed by the Levingston Shipbuilding Company, the *Cape Lookout*. But this was no ordinary ship launch. Oh no. Instead of the usual methods involving fancy greases or oils, they turned to a surprising—and very slippery—alternative: bananas. Three-and-a-half tons of "well-ripened" bananas, to be exact.

Yes, you read that right. Bananas. And not just any bananas, but bananas that were soft, squishy, and frankly past their prime. It turns out that in 1941, bananas were actually cheaper than traditional lubricants like grease, which is how the shipbuilders found themselves with literal piles of fruit ready to do the job.

But let's back up for a second. You might be wondering, *why on earth would anyone use bananas to launch a ship?* It all comes down to physics, friction, and a little bit of ingenuity. When a ship is launched, it needs to slide smoothly from the shipyard into the water. Typically, shipbuilders would use a thick coating of grease to reduce the friction between the ship and the launch rails. But in the middle of World War II, materials were in short supply, and grease wasn't cheap. Enter the banana—nature's perfectly slippery fruit.

The idea to use bananas wasn't as crazy as it might sound. After all, anyone who's ever seen an old cartoon knows that stepping on a banana peel is the classic setup for a pratfall.

The oils and sugars in bananas break down into a slimy, frictionless mush—perfect for getting a ship to slide gracefully into the sea. Plus, bananas were in abundance and dirt cheap, especially in Texas, where they could be imported in bulk from Central and South America.

So, on the morning of the launch, the workers at the shipyard began dumping mountains of ripe bananas onto the rails. You can just picture it: crates and crates of the soft, yellow fruit being spread under the enormous hull of the *Cape Lookout,* turning the shipyard into a scene more fitting for a grocery store than a military shipyard. Workers probably had a hard time holding back their laughs as the ground beneath the ship turned into a giant, sticky banana mush.

With everything in place, the big moment arrived. A crowd had gathered to watch the launch, and there was undoubtedly a little nervous tension in the air. Would the bananas do their job? Or would the ship just sit there, as confused onlookers watched three-and-a-half tons of fruit go to waste?

The horn sounded, the signal was given, and the *Cape Lookout* began its descent down the slipway. And what happened next was nothing short of remarkable. The ship glided down the rails as if it were on a cloud of butter (or, in this case, bananas). It moved so smoothly, in fact, that some onlookers probably couldn't believe their eyes. The crowd cheered as the massive vessel slid gracefully into the water, propelled not by expensive industrial grease, but by a bunch of overripe bananas.

It was a triumph of resourcefulness, and the launch went down in history as the largest ship ever to be launched using bananas as a lubricant. For days afterward, the shipyard workers probably found themselves stepping on stray bits of fruit, maybe even joking about how they could open a smoothie bar with the leftovers.

But while the idea of using bananas to launch a ship may seem comical, it's a testament to the creative problem-solving that comes during times of crisis. The world was at war, and resources were scarce. But rather than let that stop them, the shipbuilders in Texas found a way to get the job done—and they did it in a way that people would be talking about for years to come.

In fact, the story of the banana launch has become something of a legend in naval circles, a quirky footnote in the history of shipbuilding. Years later, it's still hard not to smile at the thought of a massive cargo ship sliding into the water with the help of some slippery, squished bananas. And as far as ship launches go, it's probably one of the most memorable—after all, it's not every day that you hear about a banana-powered vessel.

After the launch, the *Cape Lookout* went on to serve during World War II, playing its part in the war effort just like the many other ships launched during that time. But while other ships were remembered for their heroic missions and brave crews, the *Cape Lookout* will always be remembered for one thing: bananas.

So, the next time you're at the grocery store and you see a bunch of bananas, just remember: these humble fruits once helped launch a 10,000-ton ship into the water. And if that doesn't make you appreciate the power of a little creativity (and a lot of bananas), then nothing will.

And who knows? Maybe someday, when grease runs out again, we'll go back to the good old-fashioned banana slide. But for now, let's leave the bananas to the breakfast table and keep the ship launches a little less fruity.

Frog Legs for Breakfast: Archie Beesley's Ribbiting Regimen

In July 1970, Archie Beesley of Birmingham, England, shared a health secret that was, shall we say, *unique*. While most people start their mornings with a cup of tea or perhaps some toast, Archie swore by something a little more... *hoppy*. Every day for 46 years, he claimed, he ate a live frog. Yes, you read that correctly—*a live frog*. And if that made you hop back in surprise, just wait—because Archie swore this was the key to his good health.

According to Archie, there was nothing better for keeping his stomach in tip-top shape than gulping down an amphibian before breakfast. He even did the math, estimating that over the years, he'd consumed more than 15,000 frogs. That's a lot of ribbit in one man's diet. But to Archie, this was as routine as brushing his teeth or tying his shoes. Frogs, he insisted, were his little miracle workers, and not once had he suffered from an upset stomach. It seemed his unusual diet had left him feeling fit as a fiddle—or perhaps a frog fiddle.

Now, before you wrinkle your nose at the thought, Archie was quick to defend his unusual menu choice. "There are thousands of people in this country who swallow oysters whole," he explained, matter-of-factly. "Oysters are live too, and they do the same work in cleaning the stomach." Archie clearly didn't see much difference between oysters and frogs — except maybe that frogs have legs, and oysters, well, they don't.

His daily routine was simple but precise. Sourcing live frogs wasn't exactly something you could do at the local grocer, so Archie had to rely on his own methods, which he kept somewhat mysterious. But no matter the weather or occasion, he never missed a day.

While others were indulging in bacon and eggs, Archie was eyeing his breakfast as it tried to hop away. One can only imagine the reactions of neighbors or passersby if they happened to catch sight of Archie popping a frog like it was an early morning vitamin.

Archie's health secret wasn't just about feeling good—it was also about proving a point. In his eyes, this wasn't some bizarre quirk; it was a natural remedy, one that kept him in prime condition. And who were we to argue with his results? After all, the man had a spotless record when it came to digestive issues, and

46 years of daily frog consumption had left him nothing short of robust.

Now, you might think such a habit would raise a few eyebrows, and surely it did. But Archie wasn't about to let anyone rain on his frog parade. He stood by his theory, noting with satisfaction that his fellow Brits were quite happy to slurp down oysters, which were just as lively, if a bit less squirmy. He was even a little smug about it. "Frogs and oysters do the same work," he'd say. And really, who could argue? He seemed to have the healthiest stomach in Birmingham.

And while it's tempting to wonder what happened to Archie after his frog-filled years, one thing's for sure: the man had commitment. Whether or not science backed up his theory, Archie lived by his own rules, with frogs as his not-so-secret weapon. And hey, as far as health regimens go, it was certainly one of a kind. So the next time someone suggests an odd health tip, just remember Archie Beesley—who ate frogs for 46 years and never skipped a beat. Or a hop.

Drive-In Opera: The Barber of Oslo (And the Parking Fiasco)

In April 1989, the Norwegian National Opera set out to prove to the world—and perhaps themselves—that "opera can be fun." Their bold plan? Host the world's first *drive-in* opera, where audiences could enjoy the classic performance of *The Barber of Seville* from the comfort of their cars, with the entire production broadcast on a giant screen in downtown Oslo.

It was a novel idea. After all, who wouldn't want to experience the dramatic highs and comedic turns of *The Barber of Seville* while reclining in their car seats, snacks in hand, opera booming from their radios? The blend of high art and drive-in culture seemed like a stroke of genius. But, as with many grand ideas, there was one small problem: Norway didn't exactly have a thriving drive-in culture. In fact, most people weren't familiar with the concept at all.

When the big night arrived, a crowd gathered—just not in the way the opera organizers had expected. Instead of pulling up in cars like a scene from an old American movie, the majority of Norwegians showed up on foot, as if they were attending an outdoor concert. People stood around, politely waiting for the opera to begin, unaware that the *entire point* of a drive-in is to enjoy it from *inside* a vehicle.

Meanwhile, for the few people who did understand the drive-in concept, there was another twist: many of the cars that showed up parked facing the wrong way. Yes, instead of positioning their cars toward the giant screen to watch Figaro's antics in full operatic glory, they somehow ended up with their windshields turned away from the stage. As a result, the drivers were left staring at the back of the screen, completely missing the action, while perhaps wondering why everyone else seemed to be having a much better time.

Despite the parking misadventures, the show went on. Those standing on foot enjoyed the performance, likely with a bit more clarity than the backward-facing cars, and *The Barber of Seville* filled the Oslo air with laughter and music. For some, the opera may have been slightly overshadowed by the novelty (and confusion) of the event itself, but that only added to the charm.

In the end, the drive-in opera may not have gone exactly as planned, but it was certainly a night to remember. It proved that, while the Norwegians might not have mastered the art of the drive-in, they certainly knew how to embrace a good time, whether on foot or in a car facing the wrong way. And if the organizers' goal was to show that opera can be fun, well, they succeeded—just not in the way they expected.

So, while the audience may not have grasped the logistics of a drive-in, they certainly got the message that opera, in all its drama and whimsy, can be just as delightful under the stars of Oslo as it is in any grand opera house. Even if half the cars were pointed in the wrong direction.

Nixon's Palace Guard: The White House Fashion Flop

❧

It's January 1970, and Richard Nixon is in the White House. The Vietnam War rages on, public trust in government is shaky, and protests are sweeping across the nation. But amid all the chaos, Nixon has one pressing concern—his White House guards' uniforms just aren't fancy enough. Yes, while juggling international diplomacy and national unrest, Nixon decided that the attire of the White House guards needed a serious upgrade.

Apparently, after seeing the elaborate and dignified uniforms of palace guards in other countries, Nixon thought, *Why can't the White House have something just as snazzy?*

What followed was, in short, a fashion disaster for the ages.

The President, wanting something that would make his White House stand out, commissioned a redesign of the guard uniforms that aimed to rival those seen at Buckingham Palace or the Kremlin. The result? A white, double-breasted tunic adorned with thick gold trim on the shoulders, paired with white trousers and black boots. But the pièce de résistance was the headwear: a tall, stiff, navy-blue shako hat with a gold medallion and a sharp, peaked front that looked like it was designed to help you find north in a snowstorm.

On paper, this uniform probably seemed like it would make the guards look grand, regal, and sophisticated. In reality, they ended up looking like extras from a low-budget historical film—or, as one critic famously quipped, "They look like they're straight out of a Lithuanian opera." And that was one of the *nicer* reviews.

When the new uniforms made their debut, they immediately raised eyebrows—and not in a good way. As the guards marched in their new getups, the public didn't see an air of authority. Instead, they saw a group of men who appeared to have been plucked straight from a high school marching band, only with slightly more confusion on their faces.

It's worth remembering that the White House guards were professionals—Secret Service agents tasked with serious duties like protecting the President and maintaining security. So, you can imagine their dismay when they were suddenly told to parade around in what could best be described as "military formal wear meets historical costume drama."

One newspaper described the uniforms as "medieval pageantry," while another suggested they were better suited for an over-the-top Christmas parade. Late-night comedians had a field day. But the real blow came when even the American public—who were busy dealing with far more pressing issues like war and civil rights—took time out of their day to collectively chuckle at Nixon's sartorial misstep. As one critic put it, "They look like extras from a Lithuanian movie."

In fairness to Nixon, his heart was in the right place. He wasn't trying to humiliate his guards; he just wanted the White House to project a little extra flair, a dash of elegance. After all, if palace guards in Europe could wear plumed helmets and ceremonial swords, why couldn't the White House have a little pageantry of its own? But while Buckingham Palace had centuries of tradition to back up its uniforms, the American public wasn't quite ready to see their guards transformed into something out of a Gilbert and Sullivan opera.

Despite Nixon's efforts to bring some royal dignity to the White House, the backlash was swift and unrelenting. Within just a few weeks, the guards—clearly unhappy with their new "fashion forward" look—began phasing out the more flamboyant elements of the uniforms. First to go were the hats. The towering shako hats, which could barely fit through doorways, were quietly retired after less than a month of service. Soon after, the white tunics disappeared as well. By February, it was as if the uniforms had never existed at all.

So, what became of these ill-fated outfits? Did they end up gathering dust in the White House basement, a reminder of a sartorial misstep? Well, not quite. In one of the more amusing footnotes to the whole debacle, the uniforms were later sold off in the 1980s—not to a museum or another government agency, but to the Meriden-Cleghorn High School Marching Band in Iowa. Yes, that's right: the very uniforms that were meant to bring royal flair to the White House ended up marching down small-town streets, playing "Stars and Stripes Forever" at halftime.

One can only imagine how those Iowa students felt, marching in the same uniforms that had once been the subject of national ridicule. But hey, at least they probably looked pretty sharp from a distance, right?

In the end, the story of Nixon's palace guard uniforms is a charming reminder that, even in the highest circles of power, things don't always go as planned. Sometimes, even the President of the United States can get a little too caught up in the pomp and circumstance of it all. And while Nixon might have hoped to bring a touch of regal sophistication to the

White House, all he ended up with was a good laugh—and some very confused guards.

So, the next time you think of White House history, spare a thought for those poor guards in their white tunics and towering hats. They may not have protected the President from an assassination attempt or solved an international crisis, but they did leave us with one of the most memorable (and funny) fashion fails in presidential history.

The Time King George V's Parrot Stole the Show

It's the 1920s, and King George V is in full royal stride. The world has just come out of World War I, the Roaring Twenties are in full swing, and the British monarchy is finding its way in this brave new post-war world. But while George V is busy running an empire, there's another member of the royal household who's making headlines in his own unique way—his parrot, Charlotte.

Yes, it's true: King George V, a man known for his serious demeanor and stern public image, had a soft spot for his feathered companion. And while the king was no stranger to the spotlight, Charlotte the parrot had a knack for stealing the show in the most unpredictable ways.

Now, let's paint the scene. King George V, a man of few words and famously dry wit, was not someone you'd peg for keeping a parrot. He was more into stamp collecting (no, really—he had one of the most valuable collections in the world), and the idea of him having a lively, chatty bird is an amusing contrast to his typically stoic public persona. But Charlotte wasn't just any parrot; she was a vibrant, cheeky African grey who had picked up more royal gossip than the average palace servant.

In those days, Buckingham Palace was a bustling place, with dignitaries coming and going, royal duties being carried out, and the occasional grand banquet thrown in for good measure. Charlotte, with her sharp beak and even sharper wit, loved being part of the action. The best part? She had a habit of imitating the king's famously gruff voice, often at the most inconvenient times.

There's one tale from a formal dinner that's been passed down through palace gossip circles. Picture this: a grand table set with the finest silverware, crystal glasses sparkling under the chandeliers, and a room full of foreign dignitaries and royal guests. King George V is seated at the head of the table, looking as regal and composed as ever, when suddenly, from a corner of the room, a voice shouts, "You old fool!"

All heads turn in shock, unsure of who could have had the audacity to insult the king in his own dining room. The guests exchange nervous glances, wondering if they just witnessed the beginning of an international incident. But then, from the other side of the room, Charlotte repeats the line with perfect comedic timing: "You old fool!" It wasn't a rebellious servant or an unruly guest—it was the king's own parrot, mimicking him with uncanny precision.

Instead of the usual royal reprimand, George V—who had likely heard this a few times before—reportedly gave a rare smile, shaking his head in amusement as his guests erupted in nervous laughter. What else could they do? Charlotte had spoken, and it's hard to argue with a bird that knows how to time a punchline.

Charlotte wasn't just known for her sharp tongue, though. She had a particular fondness for copying the royal staff's conversations, often picking up gossip from maids, butlers, and footmen. She could be heard repeating phrases like "Tea at four!" and "The king is coming!" as she flitted about the palace. One can only imagine the confusion when she occasionally announced the king's presence long before he'd actually arrived in a room, causing everyone to scramble in preparation for a royal entrance that wasn't quite happening yet.

But perhaps Charlotte's finest moment came during one of George V's famous stamp-collecting sessions. The king was known to spend hours meticulously adding to his collection, carefully placing each stamp into albums that would eventually become the envy of collectors worldwide. Charlotte, curious as ever, enjoyed perching nearby, watching the king work. And one fateful day, as George V bent over to carefully place a rare stamp into his album, Charlotte swooped down, grabbed the stamp in her beak, and flew off with it!

What followed was a scene no one would expect in Buckingham Palace: the King of England, known for his stern and serious nature, chasing his parrot around the room, demanding she return the stamp immediately. Palace staff could only watch as Charlotte, fully aware of the chaos she was causing, flapped from one perch to another, the prized stamp fluttering in her beak.

Eventually, Charlotte tired of the game and dropped the stamp, unharmed but a little worse for wear. The king, relieved to have it back, reportedly muttered something about the parrot having more personality than half the people he'd met in court that week. Whether or not that's true, one thing's for sure: Charlotte had cemented her place as a legendary figure in royal history, right alongside the king himself.

The truth is, in a palace filled with tradition, decorum, and sometimes a bit too much seriousness, Charlotte the parrot brought a little levity. She kept everyone on their toes, from the royal family to the palace staff, and showed that even a king could find joy in the unexpected antics of a mischievous pet.

So, while King George V may be remembered for guiding Britain through the aftermath of World War I and the changing tides of the 20th century, those lucky enough to be in the royal inner circle will also remember the time his parrot stole the show—whether it was by mocking him at dinner, stirring up palace gossip, or making off with one of the world's rarest stamps.

In the end, it just goes to show that even in the most serious of places, there's always room for a little bit of mischief. And sometimes, it's the feathered friends who bring the most laughter.

Arrested for Snacking: The Great Grape Caper of 1988

In April 1988, a routine grocery shopping trip turned into a bizarre ordeal for Arthur Culberth, all because of a few grapes. Picture this: Arthur and his wife were casually strolling through a Miami Winn-Dixie, doing what everyone does in a grocery store—filling their cart, considering dinner options, and, in Arthur's case, sampling a couple of grapes. It was one of those harmless, instinctive moves, the kind where you pluck a grape or two from the bag to make sure they're worth the buy. Arthur wasn't thinking much of it. After all, everyone does it, right?

But, as it turned out, this wasn't going to be one of those "grab a grape, pay at the register" moments. Nearby, an off-duty cop spotted Arthur's impromptu snack. And this officer wasn't going to let the Great Grape Incident of '88 slide. He approached Arthur, demanding that he pay for the grapes *immediately*—not when he checked out, not after finishing his grocery run, but *right now*.

Arthur, baffled by the sudden confrontation, calmly explained that he fully intended to pay for the grapes when he got to the register. Surely this was just a misunderstanding, right? Well, not quite. The officer wasn't having any of it. Before Arthur could even finish his shopping, he found himself in handcuffs, being led out of the store like some sort of master criminal. His crime? A few unpurchased grapes.

Arthur spent the night in jail over this, locked up for what can only be described as the most unfortunate snack of his life. The whole thing escalated so quickly that it seemed like a strange dream. Here he was, a man who merely wanted to buy some groceries and ended up behind bars. But, as word spread, it became clear that this wasn't some nefarious plot to pilfer produce — it was a simple case of an overeager officer and a few misunderstood grapes.

Eventually, the charges against Arthur were dropped. After all, it's not exactly a felony to sample a couple of grapes before buying them. But the incident left its mark, turning what should've been an ordinary trip to the grocery store into the infamous Great Grape Caper of 1988.

The next time you're tempted to sneak a taste of that juicy fruit while shopping, you might just think of Arthur Culberth and his ill-fated snack. Because if there's one thing his story reminds us, it's that even the simplest of snacks can sometimes get you into some pretty serious trouble—at least in Miami.

Bus Start: The Short-Lived Ride to Positivity

In March 1985, officials in St. Louis had an idea they believed would revolutionize public transportation—or at least, how people *felt* about it. The humble "bus stop" sign, they reasoned, just didn't have the right energy. After all, the word "stop" felt too final, too negative. Who wants to stop, when they can start? So, in a move toward positivity, they decided to rebrand their entire bus system by installing 1,800 brand-new "bus start" signs throughout the city.

The thinking was simple: a "bus start" sounded like the beginning of a journey, something full of possibility and forward motion. Maybe, just maybe, this change in wording would encourage more people to hop on board, eager to be part of the optimism that came with starting something new. After all, public transportation wasn't just about getting from point A to point B—it was about taking the first step toward wherever your day might take you!

And so, with confidence in their hearts and a budget to burn, the city replaced the traditional "bus stop" signs with their shiny new "bus start" counterparts. Officials eagerly awaited the results, certain that this little tweak in language would draw in new riders, turning the city's buses into a beacon of positive commuting.

But here's the thing: most people didn't get it. In fact, they were downright confused. Riders found themselves scratching their heads at these "bus start" signs, unsure whether they were supposed to be catching a bus there or perhaps starting some sort of new journey entirely. For regular commuters, the sudden change in terminology was more baffling than inspiring. Was this still a place to catch the bus? Or had something entirely new and unexplained begun?

Despite the city's best intentions, the result was a mix of bewilderment and frustration. Instead of attracting more riders, the new signs mostly served as conversation pieces— people pointing and wondering what, exactly, a "bus start" was supposed to mean. The positivity that officials had hoped would catch on seemed lost in translation, and, as it turns out, when people want to catch a bus, they really just want to know where it's going to stop.

After a year-and-a-half of lukewarm results and plenty of confused commuters, the city finally threw in the towel. The "bus start" signs, though full of hopeful energy, were quietly replaced with the good old "bus stop" signs everyone knew and understood.

And while the "bus start" experiment may not have lasted long, it's a charming reminder that sometimes, the simplest terms work best. People don't always need inspiration when they're commuting—sometimes they just need to know where the bus is going to stop.

Balloonfest Debacle: When 1.5 Million Dreams Came Crashing Down

In September 1986, Cleveland's Public Square was the site of what was supposed to be a glorious spectacle—a dazzling release of 1.5 million balloons into the sky as part of a fundraising event for the United Way charity. It was a bold, colorful, and—at least on paper—joyous plan. What could be more magical than filling the sky with millions of floating balloons, each one a symbol of hope, charity, and goodwill?

The idea was simple enough. Thousands of volunteers spent hours inflating the balloons in preparation for the big moment. Brightly colored and filling the square with anticipation, the balloons were packed into a massive mesh structure that, when released, would launch them into the heavens, creating a stunning visual feast for Cleveland and a memory for the ages.

And for a brief moment, it was beautiful. The balloons rose into the air, swirling in a rainbow of color against the skyline.

Spectators gazed upward in awe as the city was momentarily transformed into a scene out of a dream. But then, just as quickly, reality hit—and it wasn't the uplifting kind.

You see, while the organizers had focused on the grandeur of the release, they hadn't exactly thought through what would happen *next*. The weather had other plans. That day, an approaching cold front combined with rain created unexpected atmospheric pressure, preventing the balloons from rising high into the sky as intended. Instead, they hovered lower than expected, and soon began to descend—by the millions.

What was meant to be a beautiful moment of hope turned into a logistical nightmare. Balloons rained down across Cleveland and far beyond, covering the surrounding areas in a colorful but chaotic mess. Streets, waterways, and even Lake Erie were soon inundated with balloons, creating an environmental and cleanup disaster.

But it didn't stop there. The balloons made their way toward the nearby Burke Lakefront Airport, causing a significant hazard and forcing parts of the airport to temporarily shut down. Flight operations were halted as balloons drifted onto runways, creating dangerous conditions for pilots. And it wasn't just the airport—balloons interfered with rescue missions on Lake Erie, as search and rescue teams struggled to navigate through the thick clouds of colorful debris.

What had started as a charitable celebration quickly spiraled into a debacle of epic proportions. The cleanup effort was immense, as crews worked tirelessly to remove the thousands upon thousands of deflated balloons that had scattered across the city and its surroundings. What was meant to uplift spirits instead became a symbol of what can go wrong when good intentions meet poor planning.

Balloonfest '86 became a cautionary tale, a reminder that even the most well-meaning events can go awry when logistics and nature collide. While Cleveland was left with quite the mess to clean up, it also walked away with a memorable—if somewhat unfortunate—chapter in its history. As for the United Way, they may have raised awareness for their cause, but it's safe to say that no one was likely to forget the day 1.5 million balloons came crashing down on Cleveland.

Miss Kangaroo: Hopping Across the U.S. (With Some Bumps Along the Way)"

❧

In January 1952, Loretta North of Australia found herself in a rather unique position. While most beauty queens get to wear tiaras and wave from floats, Loretta was crowned "Miss Kangaroo." Her royal duties? To tour the United States with two actual kangaroos as part of a publicity campaign for the movie *Kangaroo*, starring Maureen O'Hara and Peter Lawford. Yes, you read that right.

Loretta wasn't just representing Australia's beloved marsupials—she was *traveling* with them.

It sounded like a grand adventure at first. Loretta was young, excited, and more than ready for her big break. After all, this was a chance to see America, meet Hollywood stars, and promote what was sure to be a blockbuster film. Plus, who wouldn't want to tour the U.S. with a couple of adorable kangaroos by your side?

Well, as it turned out, the tour didn't exactly go as planned.

For starters, one of the kangaroos—let's call him Joey—didn't exactly enjoy his debut in showbiz. On day one, poor Joey suddenly passed away, leaving Loretta and the team scrambling to explain the absence of a key part of their kangaroo duo. It's hard to promote a movie called *Kangaroo* when one of your stars has, well, hopped off this mortal coil. Not exactly the publicity stunt they'd been hoping for.

But the show must go on, as they say. Loretta, ever the trooper, carried on with the tour— albeit with one less kangaroo. Unfortunately, that wasn't the only hiccup. Just as the tour was gathering steam, Loretta came down with a nasty case of strep throat and had to be hospitalized. Now, if there's anything more stressful than managing a movie tour, it's doing it while running a fever and losing your voice. But Loretta wasn't about to let a sore throat get in the way of her kangaroo responsibilities, so after a brief hospital stay, she was back on her feet—though probably feeling a little less glamorous than she'd envisioned when she first accepted the title.

And then there was the remaining kangaroo. If Joey had bowed out early, his partner (whom we'll affectionately call Skippy) was still very much in the spotlight. But there was one small problem: Skippy was utterly impossible to toilet train. Now, kangaroos might be graceful creatures in the wild, but put them in a hotel room or on a movie set, and suddenly you're dealing with an entirely different set of issues. Let's just say that kangaroos aren't exactly concerned with decorum when it comes to answering the call of nature.

As Loretta tried to juggle her responsibilities—posing for photos, doing interviews, and smiling for cameras—she also had to keep a close eye on Skippy, who was prone to leaving less-than-pleasant surprises wherever he went. Hotel managers weren't thrilled. Neither were the other guests. Skippy had a habit of making himself *very* comfortable in places he wasn't supposed to, and let's just say kangaroo-proofing a fancy New York hotel wasn't part of the original plan.

Still, Loretta soldiered on. She made appearances, talked about the movie, and even smiled through the chaos of it all. After all, what's a little kangaroo mayhem when you've got a film to promote? Loretta's ability to keep her composure—despite the death of one kangaroo, her own illness, and Skippy's unruly behavior—was nothing short of heroic. She might not have signed up for a crash course in kangaroo wrangling, but she handled it like a pro.

The *Kangaroo* movie tour might not have gone down in history as the smoothest publicity campaign ever, but Loretta North's adventure certainly left a lasting impression. It was a tour full of ups and downs—quite literally, if you count the kangaroo hops. But through it all, Loretta kept her sense of humor intact, knowing that no matter how chaotic things got, she'd always be able to say, "I was Miss Kangaroo."

And as for Skippy? Well, let's just say he kept bouncing through America in his own untamed way—proving that you can take a kangaroo out of Australia, but you certainly can't take the wild out of the kangaroo.

Bob Dylan's Unlikely Nobel Prize Phone Call

Bob Dylan, the iconic folk musician who famously changed the course of popular music with his poetic lyrics and gravelly voice, has always had a reputation for doing things his own way. Whether it's his unexpected musical shifts or his famously enigmatic interviews, Dylan has never been one to follow the script. And in 2016, when he won the Nobel Prize in Literature, he stayed true to form in the most Bob Dylan way possible.

When the Nobel Committee announced that Dylan had won the prestigious award for "having created new poetic expressions within the great American song tradition," the world was thrilled—and a little surprised. It was a historic moment, marking the first time a musician had been awarded the Nobel for literature. But while everyone else was buzzing with excitement, one person seemed completely unfazed: Bob Dylan himself.

In classic Dylan fashion, after the news broke, the man himself was nowhere to be found. As the days passed, the Nobel Committee eagerly waited for a response from Dylan—any response. A simple acknowledgment, a brief "thank you," maybe a statement on how honored he was. But Dylan? Not a peep.

It wasn't that he rejected the award—he just went about his life as usual, leaving the Nobel folks scratching their heads. He performed concerts, made public appearances, but made no mention of the historic prize he had just won. Eventually, the media started to speculate: *Was he going to accept the award? Was he too cool to care?*

Weeks later, after what felt like a Nobel-level mystery, Dylan finally broke his silence. He casually mentioned the award on his website — oh, and he was honored, of course. In fact, he was so honored that, according to him, the news of winning the Nobel Prize left him "speechless." But in classic Dylan style, that speechlessness had gone on for weeks.

And then there was the issue of the award ceremony. Would he show up to accept the prize in person? Once again, Bob Dylan kept everyone guessing. Finally, just days before the ceremony, he let the committee know that, unfortunately, he wouldn't be able to attend. Dylan, true to form, had other plans — he was on tour.

But in perhaps the most Bob Dylan twist of all, he later delivered his Nobel lecture—a requirement for receiving the prize—via an unexpected medium: a 27-minute audio recording. The speech, filled with his musings on literature, music, and the blurred lines between the two, was vintage Dylan: unpredictable, profound, and a little bit mysterious.

In the end, Bob Dylan's Nobel Prize saga was less about the formality and more about what made him a legend in the first place—his refusal to be anything other than himself. Whether he's writing timeless songs or casually winning the world's most prestigious literary award, Bob Dylan does it his way, leaving us all smiling and shaking our heads in admiration.

After all, only Dylan could win the Nobel Prize in Literature and somehow make it feel like just another day in the life.

U.S. Beats Soviet in Olympic Hockey Upset

The year was 1980, and the United States was in the midst of Cold War tension, disco fever, and those questionable hairstyles that defied gravity. But something was about to happen that would lift American spirits in a way no sequined jumpsuit ever could: a bunch of scrappy college kids were about to take on the seemingly unbeatable Soviet Union hockey team at the Winter Olympics in Lake Placid.

And what followed was nothing short of a miracle. That's right—the "Miracle on Ice."

Now, if you were placing bets on this game, you would've thought the U.S. team was doomed from the start. The Soviet Union team was a well-oiled machine, having won gold in five of the last six Olympics. They were hockey royalty, practically invincible. Meanwhile, the U.S. team? Well, let's just say they were made up of a ragtag group of college players, most of whom probably had to scrape the ice off their cars themselves. Their opponents weren't just talented; they were a brick wall on skates.

But the funny thing about sports is that, every once in a while, the underdog pulls off something so outrageous that it leaves everyone—players, coaches, fans—staring in disbelief.

The U.S. team, coached by Herb Brooks, wasn't exactly expected to go far. In fact, before the Olympics, Brooks had given his young team a legendary pep talk. He didn't sugarcoat it: "You were born to be a player. You were meant to be here. This moment is yours." Translation? "Good luck out there, kids. You'll need it." But Brooks knew something everyone else seemed to overlook—these young guys were hungry, scrappy, and they didn't know how to quit.

Now, picture it: the date is February 22, 1980. The Soviet team is skating onto the ice like they've already won (because, honestly, they probably thought they had). The game starts, and as expected, the Soviets score first. Yawn. Then, something happens. The U.S. team, instead of crumbling like day-old toast, fights back. They keep skating hard, making it clear they're not just there to make the Soviets feel better about themselves.

By the end of the second period, the U.S. team is trailing by only one goal. At this point, people are starting to pay attention. Fans who were only half-watching (maybe flipping through the TV Guide, wondering what else was on) are now glued to the screen. Could it be possible?

Then comes the third period. With just 10 minutes left in the game, the U.S. team ties it up. Now, the Soviet players—those cool, collected pros—are starting to look a little rattled. And in one of the most iconic moments in sports history, U.S. captain Mike Eruzione scores to put the Americans ahead. The crowd? Pandemonium. The Soviets? Stunned.

The clock ticks down, and every second feels like an eternity. The Soviets, desperate to reclaim their dominance, throw everything they've got at the American goal, but goalie Jim Craig is a brick wall in his own right. Time seems to freeze, and with just a few seconds left, the arena erupts as the final buzzer sounds.

Cue Al Michaels, delivering one of the most famous lines in sports broadcasting history: "Do you believe in miracles? Yes!" The U.S. team had done it. They beat the unbeatable. The Soviets, masters of the ice for years, had been dethroned by a group of kids who probably couldn't even grow full mustaches yet.

But here's the thing: this wasn't even the gold-medal game. That's right—the U.S. still had to play Finland to officially claim the gold. But in that moment, none of that mattered. The victory over the Soviets was about so much more than hockey. It was a David-and-Goliath moment that felt like a win for every underdog in America, and at a time when the country was grappling with Cold War anxieties, it was a welcome jolt of national pride.

After the game, the players celebrated like they had just won the lottery. Jim Craig, wrapped in an American flag, skated around the rink looking for his dad. The team hugged, cried, and probably spent the next several days trying to process the fact that they had just pulled off the impossible. As for the Soviets? Well, let's just say they weren't thrilled.

And the legacy of that game? Oh, it's lived on in a thousand ways. From Hollywood films to commercials, the "Miracle on Ice" is a story that never gets old. The 1980 U.S. hockey team didn't just win a game; they created a moment that transcended sports. They became legends, the kind of underdogs that you just couldn't help but root for.

So, the next time you're flipping channels and stumble across a documentary about the "Miracle on Ice" or find yourself watching the Winter Olympics, just remember: sometimes, miracles really do happen. Even if they come in the form of a bunch of college kids skating circles around the greatest hockey team in the world. And if that's not a reason to believe in underdogs, nothing is.

And hey, if anyone ever tries to tell you that computers are better than humans at predicting outcomes, just remind them of February 22, 1980—when the scrappiest team on the ice proved that sometimes heart, grit, and a little bit of luck can beat even the toughest competition.

Bulletproof Noodles: The Wheat That Could Stop a Bullet

In September 1984, Larry Rogers, a researcher from Salinas, California, made an announcement that sounded like it came straight out of a science fiction novel: he had accidentally invented *bulletproof wheat*. Yes, you read that correctly—wheat, the humble grain that usually becomes bread or pasta, had been transformed into something that could literally stop a bullet from an M16 rifle.

Larry wasn't your average scientist tinkering away in the lab. He had been experimenting with a mixture of bacteria and grain waste in search of new sustainable uses for agricultural byproducts. Little did he know that he was about to stumble onto a breakthrough so unexpected that it made people rethink everything they thought they knew about wheat. In one of his tests, Larry found that when hardened, this wheat mixture could stop bullets. Yes, bullets. The kind fired from military-grade rifles. Suddenly, wheat wasn't just food; it was a potential super-material.

But Larry didn't stop at its bulletproof properties. Oh no, this wheat had a whole range of possibilities. Imagine building houses out of bulletproof wheat, strong enough to withstand whatever life throws at it. And as a bonus, if you got hungry during construction, you could just whip up some noodles. Because, as it turns out, even in its reinforced form, the wheat was still perfectly edible. In fact, Larry assured everyone that it made a pretty tasty noodle—strong enough to stop a bullet, yet delicate enough to swirl around your fork in a bowl of marinara sauce.

The discovery left people scratching their heads in equal parts awe and amusement. Could the future of building materials really be as simple as the wheat we'd been eating for thousands of years? Larry's invention wasn't just a game-changer for agriculture but for the construction industry, and possibly even the military. A house built out of bulletproof wheat could withstand attacks and double as a delicious emergency food supply. Talk about multi-functional!

While the world marveled at the possibilities, Larry stayed humble, explaining that this was merely a happy accident. He hadn't set out to create bulletproof grain—he was just trying to solve agricultural waste problems. But as with many of science's greatest discoveries, sometimes the most incredible breakthroughs come when you're not even looking for them.

So, while we may not have entire cities built from bulletproof spaghetti just yet, Larry's discovery remains a quirky and fascinating reminder that sometimes, the most ordinary materials can do extraordinary things. And next time you sit down to a bowl of pasta, you might just wonder: could these noodles stop a bullet?

Well, maybe not, but in Larry Rogers' lab, anything was possible.

Operation Decoy: Lipstick, Heels, and a Side of Justice

❦

In August 1962, New York City found itself rolling out a unique and somewhat puzzling approach to catching muggers. The plan, dubbed *Operation Decoy*, involved male police officers patrolling the streets at night while dressed as women. Picture it: burly officers in lipstick, heels, and wigs, strolling through the city's shadowy corners as if they were simply out for a late-night walk. But these weren't your everyday city-dwellers—

they were bait, specifically designed to lure in would-be muggers.

The idea, while certainly creative, left many scratching their heads. Why go through the trouble of getting men into dresses and high heels when policewomen could have easily filled the role? After all, New York's police force wasn't short on brave women capable of handling the job. But for reasons never fully explained, the powers-that-be decided it was the men's turn to slip into some stockings and take on the streets in disguise.

And so, Operation Decoy was born. The male officers, with their newly acquired *feminine charm*, patrolled the streets, while a team of detectives kept close behind, ready to pounce the moment a mugger made their move. The theory was simple: muggers, targeting what they assumed were vulnerable women, would get a surprise far bigger than their wallets. And it worked, at least in part—plenty of unsuspecting criminals found themselves in handcuffs after going after a "woman" who turned out to be a very well-disguised cop.

But the operation wasn't without its challenges. Walking in heels is no easy task, even for the most practiced of feet, and the male officers quickly learned this the hard way. There were reports of officers stumbling, tripping, and generally struggling to keep up appearances while maintaining their balance. Lipstick smudges and wig malfunctions aside, the operation became something of a spectacle, both for the officers involved and for the curious New Yorkers who caught sight of these undercover efforts.

Despite the unconventional approach, the mission wasn't without its successes. A number of muggers were caught, perhaps too focused on their potential victims to notice that the wig wasn't quite sitting right or that the heels were wobbling a bit more than usual. For the criminals, it was a lesson learned: sometimes, the damsel in distress isn't what she seems.

Operation Decoy didn't last forever, and eventually, more traditional methods—along with the logical use of actual policewomen—took over. But for a brief period in 1962, New York City's streets were patrolled by men in heels, ready to bring justice in the most unexpected of ways.

In the end, the operation left New Yorkers with a story for the ages—one that involved grit, creativity, and a whole lot of uncomfortable shoes.

FDR and the Hot Dog Diplomacy

When you think of Franklin D. Roosevelt, images of wartime leadership and fireside chats may come to mind, but one of the most charming, and downright fun, moments of FDR's presidency involved something far more casual: a good old-fashioned American hot dog.

The year was 1939, and the world was on the brink of war. But before the U.S. got fully embroiled in the global conflict, FDR was tasked with entertaining one of the most important and prestigious guests to ever set foot in the White House — King George VI of England. It was a big deal; this was the first time a reigning British monarch had ever visited America, and the event was meant to strengthen the ties between the two nations.

Now, when you're hosting royalty, you might think the menu would include something like caviar, lobster, or a multi-course banquet with dishes no one can pronounce. But Roosevelt, ever the down-to-earth president, had a different idea in mind. He wanted to show King George VI a taste of real Americana. So, what did he do? He threw a picnic. And on the menu? Hot dogs.

Yes, you read that right. At Hyde Park, FDR's family estate in New York, the President of the United States served the King of England hot dogs on a casual afternoon in June. Talk about taking diplomatic relations to a new, *delicious* level.

It was an event that stunned the press. Royal visits were normally filled with pomp, circumstance, and formality, so the idea of serving the King a hot dog raised more than a few eyebrows. But FDR, with his signature charm, knew exactly what he was doing. He wanted to show that America was different—more relaxed, more approachable, and, yes, sometimes more fun than its European counterparts.

As for King George? He was a good sport. With Queen Elizabeth (the Queen Mother) by his side, he gamely picked up the hot dog and gave it a try. Reportedly, the King asked, "How do you eat it?" and FDR, not missing a beat, showed him the ropes. Whether or not the King added mustard or ketchup remains a mystery, but one thing is for sure—he enjoyed the picnic.

The press called it "Hot Dog Diplomacy," and it worked. The picnic not only cemented a strong personal bond between FDR and King George VI but also showed the world that America had its own unique brand of hospitality—one that could blend informality with important state business. And let's be honest, who wouldn't love a diplomatic meeting that includes a grilled frankfurter?

In the end, FDR's hot dog diplomacy proved that even in the most serious of times, a little fun, a little food, and a lot of personality could go a long way in forging friendships that would last a lifetime. After all, when the leader of the free world hands you a hot dog,

you take it with a smile.

The Café Where Robots Brew Your Coffee

In the bustling city of Tokyo, where innovation meets tradition at every turn, there's a café that's taking coffee culture to a whole new level—by handing over the barista duties to robots. Yes, at *Henn-na Café* (which translates to "Weird Café"), located in Tokyo's Shibuya district, you can grab your morning coffee from a robot, and it's every bit as futuristic as it sounds.

Imagine walking into a sleek, modern café, ordering your favorite cup of joe from a touchscreen kiosk, and watching as a robot with smooth, precise movements goes to work, brewing the perfect coffee. No small talk, no need to ask for extra sugar—this robotic barista, named "Sawyer," handles everything with calm efficiency. It grinds the beans, tamps the espresso, steams the milk, and delivers the final product, all while you watch through a clear window.

The café's owners wanted to solve a common problem in busy cities—long lines and overworked baristas during the morning rush.

So, why not bring in a robot that can work tirelessly, never getting tired or stressed? And, of course, being Japan, it's not just about function; it's about experience. Watching Sawyer make your coffee is a mini-show in itself, with its robotic arm mimicking the fluid motions of a human barista—minus the occasional spilled milk or crooked pour.

Despite the high-tech setup, Henn-na Café doesn't lose the personal touch. The café is still designed to be a welcoming place where you can relax, enjoy the ambiance, and sip your coffee while surrounded by both locals and curious tourists alike. In fact, many customers love coming just for the novelty of it—after all, how often do you get to say your coffee was made by a robot?

But here's the best part: the coffee is *actually* good! It's not just a gimmick; Sawyer is programmed to ensure each cup is brewed with precision, from espresso shots to lattes, down to the perfect frothy cappuccino.

While this might sound like a glimpse of the future, in Tokyo, it's just another fun, innovative way to blend technology with daily life. The café proves that robots aren't just for factories or labs—they can make a mean cup of coffee, too.

The Day a Computer Beat a Chess Champion

It was the mid-1990s, a time when pagers were still cool, the internet was slowly worming its way into homes, and computers were clunky, beeping machines that mostly handled simple tasks like word processing or rudimentary video games. But deep in IBM's research labs, something much more impressive was brewing—an artificial intelligence program designed to challenge the very limits of human intellect: chess. And not just any chess player, but the world's best.

Welcome to the story of Deep Blue vs. Garry Kasparov, a showdown that would go down in history as the day a machine took on the reigning chess champion—and won.

Now, Garry Kasparov wasn't just any chess player. By 1997, he was considered the greatest of all time, a grandmaster who had held the world title for over a decade. He was known for his aggressive style of play, razor-sharp focus, and mind that could calculate strategies several moves ahead. Some even called him the "human computer" for his ability to think through chess positions at lightning speed. So, the idea of a mere machine challenging him? Well, that was downright laughable.

Enter Deep Blue. Developed by a team of engineers at IBM, Deep Blue was no ordinary computer. It was specifically designed for one purpose: to play chess at the highest level possible. Capable of evaluating 200 million chess positions per second (yes, you read that right), it could sift through countless strategies in the blink of an eye, weighing the pros and cons of every possible move. It wasn't exactly a friendly desktop PC; this thing was a hulking supercomputer.

The stage was set. It was man versus machine, and the world was watching.

Their first battle took place in 1996, and to everyone's relief, Kasparov came out on top. Sure, Deep Blue managed to win a single game, but Kasparov dominated the match overall, as everyone had expected. The human mind, with all its creativity and instinct, still had the edge. Kasparov even quipped afterward, "I could feel human intelligence across the table."

But IBM wasn't about to pack up and call it a day. No, they went back to the lab and upgraded Deep Blue, making it faster, smarter, and, well, even more of a headache for Kasparov. The rematch was set for May 1997, and this time, Deep Blue wasn't going to play nice.

From the get-go, things felt different. In Game 1 of the rematch, Kasparov was his usual brilliant self, defeating Deep Blue with strategic flair. But then, something strange happened. In Game 2, the machine made a move so subtle, so human-like, that it spooked Kasparov. Instead of a predictable, cold calculation, Deep Blue played with what looked like intuition. Kasparov was rattled. He later admitted that the move "unsettled" him, causing him to lose the game—and more importantly, his confidence.

What Kasparov didn't know was that this "brilliant" move may have been a glitch, a random hiccup in Deep Blue's programming. But by the time Game 2 was over, Kasparov was already in his own head. He spent the next few games second-guessing himself, trying to outthink a machine that didn't get tired, didn't make mistakes, and didn't experience the pressure of performing in front of millions of eyes.

By Game 6, the final match, the tension was palpable. The score was tied, and Kasparov was starting to unravel. Whether it was the machine's seemingly "human" moves or his own frustration, Kasparov played recklessly, making errors that the world's best chess player would never normally make. Deep Blue, meanwhile, was cool as a cucumber, and by the end of the game, the unthinkable had happened: the computer won.

Deep Blue had officially defeated Garry Kasparov, marking the first time a computer had ever beaten a reigning world chess champion in a full match. It was like something out of a science fiction novel, but this was no fantasy—this was real life. The victory sent shockwaves through the world. Was this the beginning of machines overtaking humans in intellectual pursuits? Would computers one day outthink us in every domain? Headlines blared with existential questions about artificial intelligence and the future of human superiority.

Kasparov, meanwhile, was not happy. He accused IBM of cheating, insisting that human intervention must have been involved. But IBM denied any foul play, and the match went down in history as a triumph for technology. Deep Blue was retired shortly afterward, its mission accomplished. It didn't need to play any more matches—its place in the history books was secured.

But while Deep Blue's victory was a huge moment for AI, the story isn't just about a machine beating a human. It's about what it means to compete against something that doesn't think or feel the way we do. Chess, at its core, is as much a psychological battle as a tactical one, and for Kasparov, playing against an opponent that didn't feel pressure or fear was like stepping into a whole new arena. The machine didn't get flustered, didn't miscalculate under stress, and didn't care about the applause or the cameras.

Still, Kasparov's defeat wasn't the end of human dominance in chess. Since then, computers have indeed gotten better, but chess remains a game of skill, intuition, and creativity—qualities that, even today, the best players still bring to the board. And as for Kasparov? He's still one of the greatest players to ever live, and his match against Deep Blue only added to his legend.

So, the next time you fire up a chess app on your phone or challenge your computer to a quick game, just remember: there was a time when even the best human players thought, "Hey, I can take this machine on." And in 1997, the machine had other plans.

A Name for the Ages: The AMC Building's Bold Identity

❧

In 1973, the Army Materiel Command (AMC) was on the brink of a big move. Their shiny new headquarters was ready, and naturally, they wanted to make a grand entrance by giving the building a name that would reflect the cutting-edge innovation and strategic brilliance of the AMC. So, they did what many organizations do when looking for inspiration: they held a contest. With a Contest Committee to Name the New

Building in place, they eagerly awaited the flood of creative, bold, and forward-thinking ideas that would surely define their new space.

And flood in they did—524 entries, to be exact. Employees from all over submitted their best ideas, no doubt brainstorming catchy names that could rival the most iconic buildings in the country. Perhaps something like "Strategic Command Center" or "Materiel Mastery Headquarters" would give it the gravitas the building deserved.

But as the committee sifted through the hundreds of submissions, poring over each suggestion with the kind of seriousness reserved for only the most important of decisions, one entry stood out. It was simple, to the point, and in its own way, utterly brilliant. The name? **AMC Building**.

Yes, after hundreds of creative submissions, the committee landed on the very same name that was already emblazoned on everyone's paperwork: the AMC Building. They must have had quite the laugh as they realized that the best choice for the new, modern headquarters was to call it exactly what it was. No frills, no fancy titles—just straight-up honesty.

The genius behind this stroke of simplicity was none other than Francis Sikorski, an employee who likely approached the contest with a good dose of practicality. While others may have been racking their brains for something groundbreaking, Francis kept it refreshingly direct. "Why overcomplicate things?" he probably thought. And really, who could argue with that logic?

For his winning submission, Francis was awarded a $100 prize—likely with a wink and a handshake for his straightforward suggestion. And while it may not have been the most poetic or visionary name, it certainly had a charm all its own. There was no confusion, no ambiguity. The AMC Building was exactly what it said on the tin.

So, on that day in 1973, the Army Materiel Command made history in the simplest way possible. Hundreds of suggestions had been boiled down to the most obvious one, and yet it was the perfect fit. After all, sometimes the most clever thing you can do is call it like you see it.

Francis Sikorski's legacy lived on in that building, not just for his $100 prize, but for reminding us that sometimes the best solution is the one staring us right in the face. So next time you find yourself overthinking something, remember the AMC Building— proof that, sometimes, keeping it simple is the smartest move of all.

How "The Twilight Zone" Almost Didn't Get Made

In the late 1950s, American television was a land of predictable sitcoms, westerns, and safe variety shows. But one man, with a sharp mind and a penchant for unsettling tales, was about to introduce something completely different—a strange, eerie new show that would explore the outer limits of human imagination. That man was Rod Serling, and his creation, *The Twilight Zone*, would become a cultural touchstone. But here's the kicker: it almost didn't happen.

Rod Serling wasn't your typical Hollywood writer. Sure, he had the looks of a leading man and a voice smoother than a jazz record, but he was also a serious thinker. By the time he started working on *The Twilight Zone*, Serling was already known for tackling controversial social issues—war, race, politics—through his scripts. But the networks, always fearful of alienating viewers, weren't so keen on his bold ideas. They wanted entertainment, not thought-provoking messages wrapped up in heavy moral dilemmas. And so, Serling found himself at a crossroads.

You see, Serling wanted to write about the human condition, but he needed a way to slip these messages past the censors. His solution? Disguise them as science fiction and fantasy. After all, who could object to a story about a robot who wants to be human, or a man who trades places with an alien? Surely, if he wrapped his hard-hitting themes in supernatural packaging, the powers-that-be wouldn't bat an eye. And so, the idea for *The Twilight Zone* was born.

But pitching the show was no walk in the park. Network executives didn't understand the concept. A show that was a mix of science fiction, horror, and moral storytelling? It didn't fit into any of the neat categories they were used to. This was an era when TV shows had clear formulas—cowboys and gunfights, comedies with laugh tracks, or feel-good variety shows hosted by the likes of Ed Sullivan. A show that mixed genres and aimed to leave viewers uneasy? That was a gamble.

In the boardrooms of CBS, Serling's pitch was met with raised eyebrows. "Rod," they might have said, "you want to make a show where, one week, a man's stuck in a time loop, and the next week, we've got a woman convinced the world's gone crazy because no one remembers who she is?" The execs weren't sure anyone would watch something that sounded so… weird.

Serling, however, wasn't deterred. He knew his concept was groundbreaking, so he decided to shoot a pilot episode called "The Time Element" in 1958. In it, a man dreams he's transported back to Pearl Harbor the day before the infamous attack, but no one believes his warnings. The episode was haunting, unsettling, and way ahead of its time—exactly what Serling had envisioned. But CBS shelved it. They didn't think the American public was ready for something so unconventional.

It wasn't until the pilot was aired on *Westinghouse Desilu Playhouse,* as a one-off special, that things changed. Viewers were intrigued—no, fascinated—by this mind-bending story. The response was so positive that CBS executives finally began to see what Serling had been talking about all along. Maybe, just maybe, there was an audience for a show that didn't fit neatly into a box. A year later, in 1959, *The Twilight Zone* debuted, and television was never the same.

But even after it aired, there were still struggles. Early episodes like "Where Is Everybody?" (about a man who believes he's the last person on Earth) and "Time Enough at Last" (where a bookworm survives a nuclear apocalypse only to have his glasses break) were praised by critics but didn't immediately draw massive ratings. Audiences were still getting used to a show that challenged them to think, to question reality, and to feel a little uncomfortable in the process. CBS, meanwhile, kept a close eye on the numbers, wondering if Serling's strange vision was worth the investment.

Serling, always the fighter, didn't just write his scripts—he produced and hosted the show, delivering those now-famous opening lines that set the tone for each episode. "You are about to enter another dimension," he'd say in that unforgettable voice, "a dimension not only of sight and sound, but of mind." Week after week, Serling gave the audience a window into a world where nothing was quite as it seemed, where even the simplest situation could turn on its head with a chilling twist.

The network may have doubted him, but Serling's storytelling quickly caught on. By the end of its first season, *The Twilight Zone* had earned a dedicated fanbase, drawn in by the show's unique mix of suspense, science fiction, and social commentary. Whether it was a man haunted by a ventriloquist dummy or a society that controlled people's appearance and identity, each episode was a rollercoaster ride into the unknown.

The show's brilliance was in its ability to take everyday fears and amplify them into fantastical scenarios, all while making sharp, often satirical, observations about humanity.

War, paranoia, conformity—these were recurring themes, but wrapped in imaginative tales of aliens, time travel, and mysterious figures lurking just out of sight. In *The Twilight Zone,* Serling found a way to talk about things that mattered while entertaining people with thrilling stories.

And the rest, as they say, is history. *The Twilight Zone* ran for five seasons, becoming one of the most influential shows in television history. Its episodes are still studied, referenced, and imitated, proof of the lasting power of Serling's groundbreaking idea. But let's not forget: none of it would have happened without Rod Serling's persistence and the willingness to take a risk on something a little weird, a little unsettling, and a whole lot ahead of its time.

So, the next time you enter the strange world of *The Twilight Zone*, remember: it almost didn't exist. If not for one man's determination to explore the darker corners of the human mind, we might have missed out on one of television's greatest gifts—a place where imagination runs wild, and nothing is ever quite as it seems.

A Papal Miracle: The Case of the Accidental Blessing

In May 1984, a crowd gathered in Vatican City for the chance to receive a blessing from Pope John Paul II, a moment so revered that people traveled from all corners of the world to witness it. Among the sea of pilgrims and believers was a man named Jan Lavric, who, despite appearances, had no plans to be the center of attention that day. Yet, fate had a different idea.

You see, Jan was fully able-bodied, but when he arrived at the Vatican's audience chamber, there was a small problem: there were no seats left. Anywhere. As he looked around the packed room, he spotted a wheelchair nearby, left unoccupied. Figuring it was the only option if he wanted to sit, he casually parked himself in it. No big deal, right? Little did Jan know, he was about to find himself on a one-way trip to what appeared to be a *miracle.*

As the ceremony unfolded, something unexpected happened: one of the Swiss Guards noticed Jan sitting quietly in the wheelchair. Without a word, and with all the precision you'd expect from someone in full ceremonial armor, the guard wheeled Jan right to the front of the room, directly in front of Pope John Paul II himself.

The Pope, known for his warmth and grace, offered Jan a heartfelt blessing. The crowd watched in awe. There he was, seemingly a man in need of divine intervention, receiving a personal moment with the Holy Father. Surely, this was a day of significance for Jan— and perhaps something much bigger was about to unfold.

After receiving the blessing, Jan was wheeled back to his original spot, where the watching crowd's curiosity reached its peak. Then, to everyone's amazement, something incredible happened. Jan, who had just been wheeled forward, suddenly stood up, folded the wheelchair, and casually walked off with it in hand. The crowd gasped. "It must be a miracle!" someone whispered in awe. After all, they had just witnessed a man seemingly healed by the Pope's blessing.

But miracles, as it turns out, aren't always what they seem.

In the midst of the excitement, Jan had to explain the truth. There had been no miracle, no divine healing. The only thing out of place was his own embarrassment. Jan was perfectly healthy. He'd simply taken the wheelchair because it was the last available seat, and when the Swiss Guard swooped in, he was far too flustered to explain that he didn't need to be wheeled anywhere. After all, how do you tell a Swiss Guard in full uniform to stop mid-push? He figured it was easier to just go along for the ride—literally.

The story spread quickly, and while there may not have been a miracle that day, there was plenty of laughter and good-natured ribbing. Jan became an accidental legend, the man who had turned an empty seat into a papal event. In the end, he was left with a story for the ages—one that he could share at dinner parties for years, with the punchline, "Well, it wasn't quite a miracle, but it sure was a seat I'll never forget."

So, while the crowd may have hoped to witness a divine intervention, what they got instead was a delightful reminder that sometimes, life's most memorable moments come from the simplest mix-ups. After all, if you can't laugh about accidentally getting blessed by the Pope in a wheelchair you didn't need, what can you laugh about?

The Chaos of the First Super Bowl

❧

It's hard to imagine now, but back in 1967, the Super Bowl—the juggernaut of American sports that now draws millions of viewers from across the globe—was barely a blip on the radar. In fact, the very first Super Bowl, held on January 15, 1967, wasn't even called the "Super Bowl." Officially, it was known as the AFL-NFL World Championship Game, a rather dry title for what we now know as the greatest spectacle in American sports. And while today's Super Bowl is all glitz, glamour, and exorbitant commercials, the first one was... well, a bit of a hot mess.

The game took place at the Los Angeles Memorial Coliseum, a venue with seating for over 90,000 people. Surely, this inaugural showdown between the NFL's Green Bay Packers and the AFL's Kansas City Chiefs would pack the stadium, right? Wrong. Despite being the "biggest game" of the year, more than 30,000 seats were left empty. The camera operators were practically begging fans to sit closer to the field so the stadium wouldn't look so deserted on television.

Tickets, by the way, cost just $12 (which, adjusted for inflation, is still peanuts compared to today's sky-high prices), but the interest just wasn't there yet. Football was popular, sure, but the idea of a grand championship game was still in its infancy.

To make matters even more awkward, there was a network feud brewing behind the scenes. You see, both CBS and NBC had the rights to broadcast the game—CBS because they covered NFL games, and NBC because they handled the AFL. So, in a rare moment of network rivalry, both broadcasters set up shop to simultaneously broadcast the same event. This led to some delightful chaos. First, each network had its own announcers calling the game, with one channel barely able to hold back their bias for the NFL's Packers while the other was clearly rooting for the Chiefs.

Even better, the halftime show, a now-legendary affair filled with mega-celebrities and jaw-dropping performances, was far from the spectacle we know today. Instead of star-studded pop concerts, the first halftime featured two marching bands: one from the University of Arizona and the other from Grambling State University, along with a group of trumpeters known as the "Al Hirt Band." There were also 300 pigeons released into the sky, presumably to add some excitement, though reports suggest many of the birds were less interested in flying and more concerned with staying in the stadium, probably as confused as the fans.

The chaos wasn't limited to the stands or the broadcast booths. A moment of pure comedy came late in the game when NBC, realizing it had missed the opening kickoff after cutting to a commercial break too early, asked the officials to *redo* the kickoff so they could capture it for the broadcast. Yes, that's right—

there was a do-over of the most important play in football because a commercial ran long. Can you imagine trying that in today's Super Bowl? The internet would implode!

As for the game itself, it wasn't the nail-biting showdown many expected. The Green Bay Packers, led by legendary coach Vince Lombardi, dominated the Kansas City Chiefs with a final score of 35-10. The game was lopsided, to say the least, and by the end, fans were probably more focused on getting home than watching the Packers hoist the trophy (which wasn't even called the Lombardi Trophy yet—that came later). Lombardi, known for his fiery speeches and relentless pursuit of perfection, reportedly used the victory as a way to show the world that the NFL was superior to the AFL, even though the league merger was still in its early days.

Despite all the hiccups and awkward moments, the first Super Bowl marked the beginning of a tradition that would grow into a cultural phenomenon. But back then, it was more of a quirky footnote in sports history than the must-watch event it is today. There were no million-dollar commercials, no glitzy halftime shows, and certainly no wardrobe malfunctions—just a football game, two bickering networks, and a whole lot of empty seats.

Looking back, it's almost funny to think that this humble, chaotic beginning would one day evolve into something so monumental. Now, fans tune in for the ads just as much as the game, celebrities scramble for seats, and halftime performances are planned with more precision than some military operations. But it wasn't always Super Sunday. In 1967, it was just another Sunday, and the folks in Los Angeles who didn't show up? They probably didn't realize they were skipping the first chapter of what would become one of the biggest sporting events on the planet.

Stick Your Nose in It: The Library's Scent-Sational Card Catalog

In August 1974, the Upper Arlington Public Library in Ohio decided to revolutionize the way people found their next great read. Sure, anyone could wander into a library, look through the card catalog, and locate a book by its title or author, but where was the *fun* in that? What if, instead, you could track down a book by smell?

Enter the "Stick Your Nose in the Card Catalog" program—yes, that was its official name. The librarians of Upper Arlington came up with a truly scent-sational idea: what if you could scratch and sniff your way through the library? With around 60 different fragrances, this wasn't your ordinary card catalog. Each card in the catalog had a unique scent, and the corresponding book on the shelf had the very same scent. You didn't just find a book; you followed your nose straight to it.

And the scents? Well, they were anything but ordinary. This wasn't limited to the

predictable smells of flowers or frui
Upper Arlington wanted to make sure
literary journey was as full of surprises as
plot twists in the books themselves. You cou
wander through the catalog catching a whi
of everything from apple and chocolate to
garlic, cheddar cheese, and even pizza. Yes,
pizza. Suddenly, finding your next mystery
novel had the added bonus of making you
crave a slice.

Imagine walking into the library, perusing the
card catalog, and being greeted by the scent of
fresh oranges or the smoky aroma of a
campfire. Maybe you'd stumble across the

unmistakable whiff of roses, only to discover it wasn't leading you to a gardening book but a romance novel. Or perhaps you'd get a sniff of leather and realize you were being pulled toward an adventure story, full of daring deeds and heroic quests. Even cheddar cheese, which might seem an odd choice, could lead you to a cozy mystery with a quirky protagonist who happens to be a gourmet chef. With 60 different scents in play, the possibilities were endless—and your stomach might growl as much as your curiosity.

The goal, of course, was to make the library experience even more engaging, bringing a whole new level of sensory fun to book hunting. It was quirky, innovative, and downright whimsical. Sure, some patrons may have preferred the traditional method of locating their next read by flipping through cards alphabetically, but for those who liked a little adventure, following their nose through the library stacks was an experience unlike any other.

For anyone with a sharp sense of smell, this was a game changer. Looking for a mystery? Why not follow the trail of pine or smoke? Craving a cookbook? Ah, the unmistakable scent of garlic or pizza would lead the way. In the mood for poetry? How about a scratch-and-sniff of delicate roses or the sweet aroma of strawberries?

The program turned the library into more than just a quiet place to borrow books—it became an olfactory treasure hunt. And with scents like root beer and chocolate tempting patrons from all directions, you couldn't help but smile at the sheer playfulness of it all. Suddenly, searching for a book became an adventure, full of unexpected twists and turns, and maybe a rumbling stomach.

While it's unclear how long the "Stick Your Nose in the Card Catalog" program lasted, one thing's for sure: it left a lasting impression. It's not every day you get to track down a novel by following the scent of cheddar cheese. And even if the idea didn't stick around forever, it's a charming reminder that sometimes, the best ideas are the ones that make you stop, sniff, and smile.

So next time you walk into a library, think of Upper Arlington's fragrant innovation and remember: sometimes the best way to find a good book is to just *stick your nose in it.*

MIT's Big Chill: The Giant Icicle That Took Campus by Storm

～

In January 1960, the students of MIT decided that their campus needed something a little cooler—quite literally. You see, at the time, there was an "icicle-creating craze" sweeping across college campuses. Maybe it was the frigid New England winter, or perhaps it was just the endless search for new ways to avoid studying, but whatever the reason, icicles were *in*. And leave it to MIT students, with their engineering minds and love for a challenge, to take this trend to a whole new level—four stories high, to be exact.

It started innocently enough, with students talking about how they could create something big, something impressive, something that no one else could top. After all, this was MIT—the kind of place where solving complex math problems for fun was a weekend hobby. So, naturally, when the idea of creating the largest man-made icicle on campus came up, the challenge was met with the kind of enthusiasm usually reserved for solving quantum mechanics equations.

The plan was simple in theory: construct a giant icicle down the side of one of the dormitory buildings. But this wasn't going to be just any icicle. No, this was MIT, where everything had to be bigger, smarter, and, well, more colorful. The students concocted a way to make the icicle not only massive but also tricolored, because why have a plain icicle when you can have one that looks like an icy popsicle dangling from a building?

Using hoses, buckets, and a fair bit of science, the students worked tirelessly in the freezing cold, layer by layer, to create what would become a towering, multicolored frozen masterpiece. As the icicle grew, so did their excitement—and the curiosity of their fellow classmates. Soon, students from all over campus were coming by to see the frozen marvel hanging off the side of the dorm. It was quickly declared to be the largest man-made icicle ever created, at least by college students in the middle of winter.

For a few glorious days, the massive icicle was the talk of the campus. People took photos, marveled at its size, and even joked about what they would do if it broke free (which, thankfully, never happened). It was as if MIT had turned into its own winter carnival, complete with its very own ice sculpture—albeit one that could easily knock you out if it came crashing down.

But as with many grand experiments, this one wasn't meant to last. While the students were thrilled with their creation, campus authorities were less impressed—especially when they considered the potential safety risks. As much as they admired the ingenuity, they couldn't quite shake the image of that giant icicle turning into an equally giant weapon of destruction if it broke loose. After a few days of admiring the students' handiwork (and probably a few sleepless nights spent worrying about lawsuits), the decision was made: the icicle had to come down.

Campus officials quickly moved in to dismantle the towering icicle, much to the disappointment of the students who had poured so much effort into its creation. Safety concerns aside, there was something bittersweet about watching the giant icicle come down, knowing it had been a fleeting moment of brilliance, frozen in time— literally and figuratively.

Still, the students of MIT weren't about to let their accomplishment be forgotten. The giant tricolored icicle may have melted (or, more accurately, been forcibly removed), but it lived on in campus legend. For years, students would talk about the winter of 1960, when an icicle bigger than anything they'd ever seen hung proudly from a dormitory, if only for a short while.

And as far as college pranks go, this one was certainly one for the books. It wasn't destructive or mean-spirited—just a little icy fun. After all, when you're an MIT student, it's only natural to turn a simple icicle into a towering, multicolored engineering feat. It just goes to show that sometimes, even the coolest ideas (pun fully intended) don't always last—but the stories they leave behind certainly do.

And who knows? Maybe somewhere, deep in the heart of MIT's archives, there's still a blueprint for that giant icicle, just waiting for the right winter to come along again.

The Time a Puppy Nearly Stopped the First Moon Landing

❧

It's 1969, and NASA is on the verge of achieving the impossible: landing a human being on the moon. The tension is thick, the world is watching, and every detail is critical. But amidst the controlled chaos of the Apollo missions, there's one unlikely figure who almost stole the show—Snoopy, everyone's favorite cartoon dog. Yes, you read that right:

a *puppy* nearly stopped the first moon landing.

Now, before we get into how a cartoon dog almost disrupted NASA's grandest achievement, let's go back to the beginning. Snoopy, created by Charles Schulz for the *Peanuts* comic strip, had become a beloved figure by the late 1960s. He was known for his wild imagination, and while Snoopy spent most of his time daydreaming about being a World War I flying ace or a famous novelist, he somehow became the mascot for NASA's safety program. Why? Well, NASA figured that a familiar, friendly face could help promote safety without boring the astronauts to tears.

The idea was simple: NASA would create the Silver Snoopy Award, a prestigious honor given to employees and contractors who contributed to the success of human spaceflight missions with excellent safety and quality work. Astronauts themselves would hand out these cute little pins shaped like Snoopy in a spacesuit. It was all good fun and a clever way to keep morale high during the intense preparation for Apollo 11.

But here's where it gets interesting. Snoopy was more than just a mascot—he was everywhere at NASA. His image was on posters, patches, and even on the sides of spacecraft. Apollo 10, the mission right before Apollo 11, used "Snoopy" as the call sign for the lunar module, and "Charlie Brown" for the command module. The entire Apollo 10 crew, responsible for practicing the exact maneuvers needed for the moon landing, jokingly referred to themselves as Snoopy and Charlie Brown.

Apollo 10's mission went smoothly, and it laid the groundwork for the historic Apollo 11 mission. But in typical Snoopy fashion, things took an unexpected turn during one critical moment.

You see, when the lunar module was supposed to return to the command module after practicing a close flyby of the moon's surface, the module (a.k.a. "Snoopy") went a little haywire. For a few nail-biting moments, Snoopy started tumbling uncontrollably in space. Astronauts Tom Stafford and Gene Cernan had to act quickly to regain control. As the lunar module spun around unpredictably, you can almost imagine a mischievous, cartoon Snoopy grinning at the astronauts as they scrambled to fix the problem.

Thankfully, Stafford and Cernan managed to stabilize the module, and disaster was averted. "Snoopy" made it back safely to "Charlie Brown," and the Apollo 10 mission was a success. But for those brief, heart-stopping moments, NASA was holding its breath, wondering if a cartoon dog's namesake might sabotage the moon landing preparations. If things had gone differently, Snoopy could have set back the entire Apollo program, delaying or even jeopardizing the first moon landing.

After that little scare, NASA decided they had had enough excitement for one mission and put their focus on Apollo 11. But Snoopy wasn't going anywhere. In fact, Snoopy became a permanent fixture in the space program, and to this day, NASA continues to award the Silver Snoopy pins for excellence in safety and mission success.

When Apollo 11 finally did make it to the moon, and Neil Armstrong delivered his famous line, "That's one small step for man, one giant leap for mankind," you can bet Snoopy was somewhere back at NASA, wagging his tail in approval—probably imagining himself in a tiny space helmet, bouncing around the lunar surface.

So, while a certain cartoon beagle didn't literally stop the moon landing, the playful spirit of Snoopy left a lasting impression on NASA's most historic moments. And isn't it fitting? After all, if you're going to have a mascot for the most daring feat in human history, it might as well be a dog who always seems to be dreaming of something bigger.

In the end, Snoopy didn't stop the moon landing—he helped inspire it. From his place in the comic strips to his space-bound alter ego, Snoopy became a symbol of imagination, ambition, and a little bit of lighthearted fun in a high-stakes world of science and space exploration.

As for the astronauts, they probably had one thing on their minds after successfully landing on the moon: "Good grief, Snoopy. We made it."

Operation Sticker Shock: The Army's Pricey Experiment

In December 1951, the U.S. Army came up with an idea that was both practical and, well, a little comical in hindsight. It was called Operation Cost-Consciousness, and it was exactly what it sounds like—a plan to remind soldiers just how expensive their equipment really was. But the way they went about it was truly something special. They put price tags on *everything*. And I mean everything.

Imagine it: a tank rolling up with a sticker slapped on the side that reads "$200,000," or a rifle in a soldier's hands with a bright little tag hanging from the barrel that says, "$85." And can you picture the parachutes? Because yes, even the parachutes had price tags fluttering in the wind. As one staffer remarked at the time, "It looks just like a department store here." Only, instead of sweaters on sale, it was military-grade gear.

The thinking behind this grand experiment was simple: if soldiers knew exactly how much all their equipment cost, they'd be more careful with it. After all, it's easy to toss around a helmet like a beach ball when you don't know it costs a small fortune. But once you see that $60 price tag dangling from it, suddenly you're handling that helmet like it's made of glass.

And surprisingly, it worked—for a while. Soldiers became more cautious, more mindful of the equipment they were using. Gone were the days of throwing a wrench into the toolbox with reckless abandon or casually leaning an expensive rifle against a tree. There was a certain pride in knowing you were handling a piece of equipment worth more than your car—or at least your future car, whenever you could afford one.

But for all its successes, Operation Cost-Consciousness had its limits. You see, there's only so much awareness you can raise before it starts to lose its charm. At first, soldiers would chuckle and shake their heads when they saw the price tags. "Did you know this jeep is worth more than my house?" was a common joke around the base. But after a while, the novelty wore off, and it began to feel like the army was running a clearance sale.

There were also a few unintended consequences. Take Private Johnson, for example. The story goes that he was so overwhelmed by the $1,200 price tag on his field radio that he refused to use it for fear of breaking it. "I can't be responsible for something worth more than my entire year's salary!" he reportedly exclaimed, clutching the radio like it was a priceless artifact.

Another soldier, Sergeant Miller, became notorious for calculating the cost of every mission down to the last bullet. He'd turn to his squad mid-maneuver and say, "Do you *really* want to waste that round? That's 30 cents you're about to fire off!" His platoon joked that Miller had become more of an accountant than a soldier, but hey, they *were* saving money.

Despite the laughs and initial cost savings, Operation Cost-Consciousness was quietly shelved after about a year. There's only so much you can do to remind soldiers that their grenade launcher costs more than their salary without it becoming a little demoralizing. Plus, let's be honest, it's hard to take orders seriously when your sergeant is wearing a helmet that says "$60—Handle with Care."

Still, the operation wasn't a total loss. It left a legacy of sorts, a little reminder that even in the most serious of jobs, sometimes it's good to stop and consider the value—both literal and metaphorical—of the tools you're using. And who knows? Maybe in some forgotten army warehouse, there's still a jeep out there with its price tag attached, a relic of a time when the U.S. Army tried its hand at retail.

So next time you're handling something valuable, whether it's a brand-new smartphone or your prized collection of gadgets, remember Operation Cost-Consciousness. If soldiers could carefully tote around a $200,000 tank, you can probably keep track of your car keys. And if not, maybe slap a price tag on them for good measure.

The Mystery of the Missing Mail: A Trashy Confusion

In June 1978, the quiet town of White Plains, New York, experienced one of the more unusual bank "robberies" on record. Picture it: a large man strolls into a local bank, calm as can be, and makes his way to the teller. The atmosphere inside the bank is your typical mid-day scene—people depositing checks, cashing out, and waiting in line. But soon, things were about to get a lot more interesting.

The man approached the teller, leaned in, and demanded money. Now, this is the part of the story where most of us imagine the classic Hollywood bank heist—threats, duffel bags, and high-speed getaways. But this wasn't your typical bank robber, and this wasn't going to be a typical heist.

Without hesitation, the teller, assuming she was being robbed, handed over a bundle of cash. Better safe than sorry, right? But what happened next wasn't a quick escape. No, the man simply took the money, glanced at it, and then demanded *more.* So, with her heart likely pounding, the teller handed him another bundle of notes.

Now, if you thought this was the part where he made a run for it, think again.

Instead, the man suddenly jumped into the air, threw his arms up, and yelled, "*Wheee!*" The startled bank staff and customers blinked in disbelief as he proceeded to dance—a full-on, impromptu jig right there in the middle of the bank. This wasn't exactly the behavior of a hardened criminal. But the man wasn't done yet. As he twirled and hopped around, he joyfully exclaimed, "*When I need a little money, I know where to come!*"

And just like that, he was gone—leaving the bank, not with the bundles of cash, but with a spring in his step and a smile on his face. As the doors closed behind him, the employees and patrons were left in stunned silence, staring at the money he left behind. There had been no getaway car, no dramatic escape, just a man who seemed to have confused the bank for a stage.

The authorities were called, of course, and the man was later picked up for psychiatric observation. Turns out, this wasn't a criminal mastermind with plans to outwit the system; he was simply a fellow in need of a bit of help—and maybe an audience for his spontaneous dance routine.

The teller, probably still shaking off the odd encounter, had to laugh. There are many ways to demand money from a bank, but not many involve a celebratory dance and the words, "Wheee!" as your grand finale. In a world full of serious heists and high-stakes crime dramas, this incident was a reminder that sometimes, even in the strangest situations, you've just got to shake your head, laugh, and appreciate life's quirks.

As for the man? Well, he certainly left an impression. While he may have known where to go when he needed a little money, it seemed he was really just looking for a bit of fun. And who knows—maybe somewhere, he's still dancing his way through life, spreading smiles wherever he goes.

Hot Dog-Vertising: A Medium Rarely Used

In January 1990, the Viskase Corporation believed they had revolutionized both the culinary world and the advertising industry in one fell swoop. Their new technology, as bold as it was bizarre, allowed edible-ink ads to be printed directly onto hot dogs. Yes, you heard that right—hot dogs were no longer just the star of summer barbecues; they were now being pitched as the next big "communications medium." Forget billboards or commercials—your brand's message could now sizzle right there on someone's lunch.

The idea was certainly... creative. Viskase imagined companies printing their logos or catchy slogans onto every frankfurter, turning stadium hot dogs into valuable advertising real estate. Even better, they suggested this as an excellent way to reach children and "establish brand preference early." Because, really, what better way to create lifelong brand loyalty than by having your logo branded onto someone's snack? A happy child with mustard on their face and an ad on their wiener—now that's marketing!

But, as it turned out, not everyone was ready to jump on the hot-dog-vertising bandwagon. Despite the innovation, the company struggled to find takers for its edible ad technology. While the idea of printing messages onto food seemed quirky enough to spark interest, practical issues quickly started to pile up.

One concessions manager summed up the problem best: "Our hot dogs are already cooked, in a bun, and wrapped when they're sold. You wouldn't see the message." It turns out, the art of advertising on a hot dog was a bit trickier than anticipated. Once the hot dog was nestled into a bun and smothered in ketchup and mustard, any carefully printed logo or slogan would be hidden beneath a tasty mess of condiments. And let's face it—by the time anyone would get a peek at the ad, they'd likely be halfway through eating it. So much for establishing brand loyalty.

There were other concerns too. Imagine, for instance, trying to read an advertisement on a rapidly shrinking hot dog at a ballpark, only to find that by the time you'd deciphered half the message, it was already in your stomach.

Plus, not everyone was keen on mixing advertising with their food. "I'll have mine with ketchup, mustard, and a side of corporate messaging," said no one ever.

Despite the good intentions and the quirky charm of the idea, hot-dog-vertising failed to catch fire. Viskase had imagined a world where every bite of a hot dog carried a clever message, but in reality, people were more interested in enjoying their food than reading it.

And so, the edible-ink technology quietly fizzled out, a forgotten footnote in the annals of advertising history. But the idea still brings a smile to those who remember it—a reminder that sometimes, even the quirkiest ideas don't quite make the cut. After all, when it comes to hot dogs, sometimes it's best to just let them be hot dogs.

Because in the end, who needs an ad on their frankfurter when the real magic is in the bite?

When Elvis Presley Met Richard Nixon

It's December 21, 1970, and the King of Rock 'n' Roll is about to pull off one of the most bizarre meetings in American history. Elvis Presley, known for his swiveling hips, rhinestone jumpsuits, and gospel-fueled charisma, has decided to offer his services to none other than President Richard Nixon. And this isn't a concert request, mind you — Elvis has something much bigger in mind. He wants to help the U.S. government in the fight

Stories to Keep Seniors Sharp

against drugs. And not just any role will do; Elvis wants to be made a "Federal Agent-at-Large."

Yes, you read that right. Elvis Presley, the man who once sang about being a "Hound Dog," was ready to trade his microphone for a badge. How did this surreal scenario come about? Buckle up—it's a wild ride.

It all started when Elvis, reportedly frustrated with the counterculture movement that was sweeping America in the late '60s and early '70s, decided that he could be part of the solution. He'd grown tired of the drug culture associated with the youth rebellion, and despite the irony of his own well-documented use of prescription drugs, he felt he had something to offer the country in its battle against narcotics. And who better to offer it to than the President of the United States?

On the morning of December 21, 1970, Elvis boarded a flight to Washington, D.C., unannounced and without security detail. He was accompanied by no one but himself—and, curiously, a set of commemorative World War II pistols and a letter written on American Airlines stationary. The letter, addressed to President Nixon, laid out Elvis's desire to meet with him and his hope to be sworn in as a "Federal Agent-at-Large" in the Bureau of Narcotics and Dangerous Drugs. Elvis believed he could use his fame and influence to help fight drug abuse, especially among America's youth.

If this sounds strange, just wait—it gets better. When Elvis arrived in D.C., he didn't contact the White House through official channels. Nope, the King decided the best way to get the President's attention was to just stroll right up to the gates of 1600 Pennsylvania Avenue and drop off his handwritten letter.

Here's where things get really funny. Imagine being a White House staffer that day. You're minding your own business, checking the daily schedule, and suddenly, the King of Rock 'n' Roll's name pops up. "Excuse me, sir," a security officer might have said, "Elvis Presley is here... to see the President."

Naturally, the staff was skeptical, but one man, Egil "Bud" Krogh, a deputy assistant to Nixon, saw an opportunity. Krogh, a huge Elvis fan, decided this was worth the gamble and managed to get the meeting on the President's schedule. A few hours later, Elvis, decked out in a velvet cape, oversized sunglasses, and a gold belt, strutted into the

Oval Office for a face-to-face with Richard Nixon.

Now, picture this for a moment. Nixon, stiff as ever, sitting behind his desk in the Oval Office, looking at a bedazzled, larger-than-life Elvis Presley. The contrast couldn't have been starker. But it wasn't awkward—quite the opposite. Nixon, normally a man of cold pragmatism, seemed genuinely taken with Elvis, shaking his hand and listening intently to what the King had to say.

Elvis presented Nixon with a gift: one of those commemorative pistols he had brought along. Nixon accepted it—though, for security reasons, they made sure the gun wasn't loaded. Elvis then launched into an impassioned plea, saying that he wanted to help the country combat drug abuse and that he needed an official badge to do it. He believed that with a badge, he could go undercover and infiltrate drug circles. The idea of Elvis Presley, in full sequined regalia, going "undercover" to bust drug rings is a visual that's hard not to laugh at.

But here's the kicker: Nixon agreed. He instructed his staff to make sure Elvis got the badge he was after. Elvis was made an honorary agent in the Bureau of Narcotics and Dangerous Drugs. It wasn't an official position—he didn't get to carry a gun or go on stakeouts—but he did get a shiny badge, and that seemed to be enough for the King.

As the meeting wrapped up, Elvis couldn't resist asking for one last thing: a photograph with the President. Nixon, ever the politician, agreed. The two stood side by side, Nixon in his crisp suit, Elvis in his flamboyant outfit, posing for what would become one of the most iconic and surreal photos in American history. Today, that picture of Nixon and Elvis is the most requested photo in the National Archives, more popular than images of the moon landing or any presidential inauguration.

The story doesn't end there, though. After the meeting, Elvis happily left the White House with his badge in hand, convinced that he could make a difference. As for Nixon, he had no idea the meeting would become a pop culture legend. But the relationship didn't really go beyond that one bizarre afternoon. Elvis never did go undercover to bust drug cartels, though the idea of him kicking down doors in Las Vegas while shouting "Thank you, thank you very much" remains a hilarious fantasy.

What remains is the legacy of that moment— two icons from completely different worlds coming together in the most unexpected way. It's a story that shows just how unpredictable life can be, and how sometimes, all it takes is a little nerve, a letter, and a whole lot of charisma to get what you want.

And so, on that winter day in 1970, the King of Rock 'n' Roll left the White House with his badge, having briefly made himself part of America's war on drugs. As for Nixon? Well, let's just say he probably walked back to his desk, shaking his head, muttering to himself, "Only in America."

The Wrong Signature:
Montblanc's Dumas Dilemma

In October 1996, Montblanc, the renowned maker of luxury pens, found itself in an ink-splattered predicament of literary proportions. As part of a limited-edition series, Montblanc released a $750 pen engraved with the signature of none other than Alexandre Dumas, the legendary author of *The Three Musketeers* and *The Count of Monte Cristo*. It was a tribute to one of the greatest storytellers of all time, and surely, Dumas himself would have been honored—if it were actually *his* signature.

What Montblanc didn't realize until after these pens hit the market was that the engraved signature belonged not to the famous Alexandre Dumas *père* (father), but rather to his son, Alexandre Dumas *fils* (son). While Dumas Jr. certainly had his own literary merits—best remembered for his novel *The Lady with the Camellias*—he wasn't exactly who people had in mind when they shelled out $750 for a piece of literary history. After all, collectors were expecting the swashbuckling author who gave us musketeers, not the man behind tragic Parisian love affairs.

The mistake was as surprising as it was awkward. Imagine the disappointment of pen aficionados and literary buffs who thought they were holding the mark of a legend, only to realize they were, well, one generation off. Montblanc quickly found itself scrambling to issue a recall of the pens, which had already become hot items among collectors. To their credit, they handled it with grace, correcting the mistake and ensuring that the correct Dumas—the one wielding the quill in 19th-century adventure novels—would have his proper place on the limited-edition pen.

Of course, the story didn't end there. As with any rare mishap, the "wrong" Dumas pens became something of a collector's item themselves. After all, how often do you find a pen that commemorates one of history's great authors—but with a twist? Some collectors held on to their mis-signed pens, enjoying the unexpected trivia that came with them, while others appreciated the corrected versions that finally bore the signature of the intended literary giant.

In the world of high-end pens and literature, it's a gentle reminder that even in the most refined circles, mistakes happen. And while Montblanc may have momentarily mixed up their Dumas, they still managed to write a unique chapter in the annals of collectible history.

Because really, whether it's Dumas *père* or Dumas *fils*, sometimes a little mix-up just makes the story that much more interesting.

Thank You

Before you close this book, let's take a moment to celebrate—you've just kept your mind sharp, your heart light, and hopefully, your smile big! Whether it was a witty tale that made you chuckle or a bit of trivia that got your brain buzzing, we hope these stories brightened your day and left you feeling a little more engaged and energized.

But don't stop here! Take a moment to share the fun. If this book brought a smile to your face or a spark to your conversations, we'd love it if you could leave us a review. As a small independent company, your feedback really does make a difference. Reviews help us keep creating books like this—full of joy, laughter, and a little wisdom—to share with you and others. Plus, it helps us navigate the wild world of Amazon, where every kind word pushes us a little further forward.

So, until next time, keep smiling, stay sharp, and don't forget to throw in that witty comeback when your granddaughter checks in. You've got this!

Printed in Dunstable, United Kingdom